Kooski
A Gray Wolf

by
Bonnie Highsmith Taylor

Perfection Learning®

Photographs courtesy of Robert E. Barber: pp. 9, 10, 12, 14, 16, 21, 23, 30, 36, 48.
Some images copyright www.arttoday.com
Book Design: Randy Messer

Dedication

For Tom Strode and Kooskia, Idaho

About the Author

Bonnie Highsmith Taylor is a native Oregonian. She loves camping in the Oregon mountains and watching birds and other wildlife. Writing is Ms. Taylor's first love. But she also enjoys going to plays and concerts, collecting antique dolls, and listening to good music.

Paperback ISBN 0-7891-2844-6
Cover Craft® ISBN 0-7807-9003-0
6 7 8 9 10 11 PP 09 08 07 06 05

Contents

Chapter 1

Kooski was born on a cold spring morning. His parents had mated in mid-February. Kooski was born 63 days later.

There were six pups in the litter. Three females and three males. Some wolves have as many as ten pups in a litter. Usually there are about six.

Each pup weighed about one pound. Kooski was a little bigger than the rest.

Someday Kooski would weigh 100 pounds or more. He would be about six feet long. And stand at least 32 inches tall at the shoulder.

Gray wolves can weigh as little as 45 pounds. Some weigh well over 100 pounds. It depends on where they live. In warmer places, they are smaller. Kooski lived where it was very cold in the winter.

Kooski's father was a large gray wolf. Gray wolves can be any color. From white to buff to brown to black. But most are gray.

Kooski's father was an alpha wolf. The alpha wolf is the leader of the pack. He is usually the biggest and strongest. Other wolves treat him with honor. And even fear.

Beta wolves are next in importance. Omega wolves are at the very bottom of the pack. Omega wolves must obey all the others.

When a low-ranking wolf meets a high-ranking wolf, it tucks its tail between its legs. It whines. It may even "kiss" the face of the other wolf.

If a high-ranking wolf gives a "bossy" look, the lesser wolf will roll on its back. It seems to say, "I give up."

Kooski's mother was also an alpha wolf. She was the most important female in the pack. Even beta male wolves had to obey her. So did all low-ranking wolves.

There was still snow on the ground when Kooski was born. The wind was blowing. But Kooski and his brothers and sisters were warm and snug.

Their mother and father had dug the den where they lived. That was a few weeks before the pups were born.

The entrance to the den was about 20 inches by 26 inches. It was over eight feet deep. Some dens can be much deeper if the soil is soft.

Kooski's parents would probably dig another den later. Wolves move their babies once or twice. They feel safer changing their location.

Kooski whimpered. He snuggled closer to his mother. Her body was soft and warm.

In the darkness, Kooski searched for a nipple. How sweet the warm milk tasted. He pawed against his mother's belly. That made the milk come faster. His brothers and sisters nursed beside him.

The mother wolf licked them with her tongue. She had to keep her pups clean. She also licked the urine and feces from their bodies. Otherwise, the den would become dirty.

The pups were born with blue eyes. But they were tightly closed. They would open in about two weeks. As the wolves grew older, their eyes would turn yellow or brown.

For the first week or so, Kooski's mother did not leave the den. The father wolf brought food to her.

Kooski and his siblings were their parents' third litter. Wolves mate for life. They have a new litter every spring.

Kooski's older brothers and sisters would baby-sit the litter. Then their parents could hunt. Or take a rest from their young.

When Kooski was older, he would baby-sit the next litter. Some wolves in a pack have not mated. They also help care for the pups.

Kooski filled his tummy with warm milk. He fell asleep. One by one, all the other pups fell asleep too. The mother wolf also slept.

Chapter 2

It was a long way to the opening of the wolf den. Kooski walked toward it. His legs were still wobbly. His eyes had been open for over a week.

Outside, Kooski's father made a squeaking sound. It was a sound that the male wolf used to call his pups. Kooski moved faster. The other pups followed him. At last, all six were outside.

It was a warm day. A light breeze blew through Kooski's hair. It tickled his nose. It felt good.

His mother and father lay down. They watched as the pups tumbled in the grass.

The pups nipped at one another. They had tiny, sharp teeth. Their yelps and growls rang out as they played. Finally, the six pups tired. They fell asleep in a heap.

The mother wolf moved closer to her litter. She licked them clean as they slept.

Wolves are very good parents. The father wolf helps care for the pups. He is very protective of them.

Much affection is shown among members of a pack. A pack includes the parents and their offspring. And maybe some of their unmated relatives.

Wolves do not mate until they are two or three years old. If the food supply in the area is low, only the alpha pair mate and have pups.

Often an unmated adult wolf will leave the pack. It will find a wolf who has left another pack. They will go to an area far away. They will raise a family. And start a new pack.

Each pack has its own territory. Any wolf who enters it is at risk. The pack may kill an outsider.

Wolves mark their territory. They urinate on rocks, trees, and bushes. They will not cross a marked area. Even when chasing game.

In many places, wolves catch a lot of mice. A wolf may eat 20 mice at one time. A wolf's hearing is so sharp it can hear mice under a foot of snow.

The wolf has a strong sense of smell too. This is partly because they have wet noses. Odors are gases. So they are best noticed when mixed with the moisture on the wolf's nose. The wind helps too. When it blows in the wolf's direction.

By the time Kooski was six months old, he would hunt with the pack. Wolves hunt large game in groups of four to eight. Sometimes more.

They hunt deer, elk, moose, and caribou. They usually kill the old or weak animals. This keeps the herd healthy.

Wolves also eat birds, fish, frogs, and even berries.

Hunting large game is hard work. The pack may be successful only ten percent of the time.

A wolf can run 40 miles an hour. But it is hard to catch a large animal while running. So wolves circle their game. Then they attack from all sides.

After the kill, the wolves eat until they're full. A wolf can eat as much as 20 pounds.

They will not eat again for two or three days. Wolves who are old and sick are fed by the others.

While the pups slept, their father wandered off. The mother wolf stayed with the pups.

After a while, the pups awakened. They were hungry. They nursed.

Then the six began to tumble about again. They climbed on their mother. Kooski nipped her ears until she pushed him away.

He then pounced on a sister. A little black pup. She was the smallest of the litter. Her yips brought the mother wolf to the rescue.

The mother made a squeaking sound. A sound that meant, "Don't play so rough."

Kooski and the other pups toddled around. They chewed on blades of grass and sticks. One little male tried to catch a beetle that crawled on the ground.

The father wolf finally returned. He had eaten some mice. He spit them up on the ground. This is called regurgitating.

The pups slobbered as they nibbled the food. The mother licked the male wolf's mouth. That made him vomit again. More partly digested food came up. The pups gobbled it down.

They growled and snapped as they ate. When the food was gone, they slept again.

It had been a good day for Kooski. He had seen the great outdoors. And he had eaten his first meat.

Chapter 3

The next morning, the parents picked
the pups up by the back of their necks.
They carried them one by one. The
wolves moved to a new den.

The den was in a good place. It was in the side of a hill. And it was near a creek. They would live there for a few weeks.

Then the family would leave the den. Wolves only live in dens when the pups are small. The pups would soon move to an open area. This site would be a mile or more from the den.

While the parents hunted, the pups would be cared for by a baby-sitter. The baby-sitter could be a male or a female. Sometimes the baby-sitter is a very old wolf. One that can no longer hunt.

Kooski was growing fast. Every day, he and his brothers and sisters played outside the den.

One morning, Kooski and a sister tumbled about. They had wandered several feet from the den. The mother wolf lay not far away.

Suddenly, there was a loud scream above them. A dark shadow covered Kooski and his sister. They were scared.

Instantly, the mother wolf was there. She growled in anger. Her teeth snapped.

An eagle dove at the pups. The mother wolf saved the pups just in time. The eagle's claws had barely scratched the female's nose.

Small pups are sometimes carried off by eagles and hawks. Many pups do not live to be adults. Some die from diseases. Some are killed by hunters.

Until laws were passed, wolves were killed by the thousands. In some places, they are still hunted. Some are killed illegally.

In early America, the government started paying money for killing wolves. This is called bounty. It means reward. Some people made their living killing wolves. Their furs were very valuable also.

Early settlers hated the wolves. They dug pits to trap them. They poisoned them. They took young pups from their dens. And they clubbed them to death.

The settlers did not just hate the wolves. They were afraid of them. They thought wolves killed people.

But there are no records of healthy wolves harming people. Wolves are usually very shy. They avoid humans.

The killing of wolves went on and on. Little by little, the gray wolf vanished. From all the states but Minnesota and Alaska. And small areas of Idaho and Montana.

The red wolf, which once lived in the southeastern part of the United States, disappeared. Also the Mexican wolf from the Southwest.

In some places, wolves were trapped and infected with a disease. Then they were put back into the wild. They infected other wolves.

Later, hunting was even done from planes and snowmobiles.

The gray wolf has many names. It depends on where it lives. Or once lived.

The Arctic wolf roams the far North. The eastern timber wolf lives in Minnesota. There's the buffalo, or lobo, wolf. It once roamed the American plains.

The gray wolf's scientific name is Canis lupus. It looks like a German shepherd dog.

The scientific name of the red wolf is Canis rufus. Red wolves are the smallest wolves in North America. They weigh between 30 and 80 pounds. They are only about 16 inches high at the shoulder.

In 1976, the U.S. Fish and Wildlife Service started a Red Wolf Recovery Team. Now there are other recovery programs. They raise red wolves to be put back into the wild. So far only about 40 percent have survived.

Wolves are related to the coyote, the jackal, the dingo, and the domestic dog. The Arabian wolf is the smallest in the world. It is only about 30 inches long.

Wolves are mammals. That means they feed their young milk. They are carnivores. That means they eat meat.

Canis is the name for the ancestor of the wolf. It lived one million years ago.

There are wolves in many parts of the world. But there are no wolves in Great Britain.

Hundreds of years ago, the English began killing them off. Some of the wolves had rabies. They were dangerous to humans. In a short time, the wolves became extinct. They were never brought back.

Hunters think wolves kill too much wildlife. Others think they are important to wildlife. That they help the balance of nature.

Wolves do not kill without a reason. They kill to eat. They do not waste what they kill.

Chapter 4

One morning, Kooski woke to a strange sound. The other five pups slept soundly in the dark den.

Kooski made his way to the opening. He looked out. His mother and father were not there.

But two of Kooski's older siblings were playing. The dark gray wolf was Kooski's brother. The light buff one was his sister. They had been born the year before Kooski.

The wolves were running around and around. They chased each other. They yipped as they played. They tumbled about on the ground.

Kooski watched. He cocked his head to one side. Kooski thought it looked like fun. He decided to join them.

The young wolf took a few steps out of the den. But something was falling on his head. It was rain. That was the sound that had awakened him.

Kooski had never seen rain. He shook his head. He licked the rain off his nose.

He went toward the big wolves. The dark gray wolf stopped his play. He nuzzled his little brother. Then the big sister nuzzled him.

The older male rolled on his back. Kooski pounced on him. He tugged at his fur. He growled in his play. For a long time, they played in the rain. The older wolves were gentle with the young one.

Suddenly, from far away, there came a long, deep howl. Then another a little closer. Then several howls all together.

Kooski knew it was the rest of the pack. They were returning from their hunt.

Kooski's big brother and sister raised their heads high. They howled and howled in answer. Kooski howled too. He threw back his head. The sound that came out was not very loud. But it was his first howl.

The other pups came out of the den. They had heard the howling of the pack.

The rain had almost stopped. The pups yawned and stretched. They sniffed the air. They all knew the smell of their parents.

The pack reached the den area. The pups ran toward the mother wolf. They licked her lips to make her vomit. Up came the meat she had swallowed. The pups snarled at one another as they gobbled their food.

The pack had killed a deer. They had
eaten their fill before returning. Now the
two wolves who had baby-sat the pups
took off. They followed the trail to the
dead deer. They ate what had been left for
them.

Wolves are very loyal to the other wolves in the pack. They will defend a weaker wolf against an outsider. They will make sure they are all fed. Even the sick.

Sometimes a lone wolf will be let into the pack. But his rank will be very low. At least until he proves himself.

A lone wolf may be one that has been driven away from another pack. Maybe for not obeying the lead wolf. Or maybe it left because it was picked on by the others.

When an alpha wolf gets old and dies, a younger wolf becomes the leader. Usually a beta wolf.

Kooski and his brothers and sisters filled their tummies. Now it was nap time. Wolves usually take naps after eating.

The sun came out. It was warm. The air was fresh and clean after the rain. The other two wolves returned. They, too, were full. The wolf pack slept.

Chapter

At last, Kooski and his siblings left
the den. The new home was about a mile
away. It was a large clearing. There were
trees around it. The clearing covered
about an acre.

All the members of the pack used the
new site. They slept in the open. If the
nights were cool, they would curl up.
They would tuck their noses between
their legs. And cover their faces with their
furry tails.

In winter, wolves sleep this way on top
of the snow.

On chilly nights, Kooski and his brothers and sisters snuggled together.

Wolves feel safer sleeping in open areas. The only escape from the den is the opening.

The wolf's coat is so thick it holds body heat. Even at -50°, a wolf will sleep outdoors. A wolf's footpads stay at just above freezing temperature. This also helps them stand the cold.

In many fairy tales and folktales, the wolf is an evil villain. In *Little Red Riding Hood*, the wolf eats the grandmother.

In *The Three Pigs*, he destroys the pigs' homes. And tries to eat them. The wolf eats the baby goats in *The Wolf and the Seven Kids*.

In Native American legends, the wolf is a hero. He is not an enemy. Many Native American people say the wolf is a teacher. He teaches loyalty, sharing, and strong family values.

There is an old legend of an Indian brave and a wolf.

One day a brave was returning to his camp. He had killed a deer. He was carrying the deer over his shoulder. On the trail, he saw a wolf. The wolf was very thin.

"Ah, my friend," said the brave. "There is much game in the forest. Yet, you look hungry."

The brave cut a chunk of meat from the deer. But the wolf did not take it. The wolf panted and slobbered.

The brave put down the deer. He carefully opened the wolf's mouth. A bone was stuck in his throat.

"Ah, my brother," said the brave. "This is the problem."

He removed the bone. The wolf gulped down the meat. Then he licked the brave's hand and walked off.

Many months later, the brave was hunting in the forest. The wind began to blow. It blew very hard. A tree fell and knocked the brave to the ground. It fell across his body.

He was pinned tightly. For hours and hours, he struggled. But he could not free himself.

All at once, a large wolf appeared. It was the wolf the brave had helped. The wolf began to dig. He dug and dug under the fallen tree. At last there was room for the brave to crawl out.

"Thank you, brother," cried the brave. "I will never forget you."

Many Native Americans honor the wolf in dances and ceremonies. Some have used its name for their own.

By fall, Kooski was nearly as large as his father. He had gone on hunts with the pack.

Sometimes he and one or two of his siblings would go hunting together. They would catch rabbits or birds.

Early one morning, Kooski and a brother left together. They went a long way in search of game.

They were bounding through a
clearing. All at once, a loud sound rang
out. Then another. Kooski's brother fell
to the ground. Blood spurted from his
neck.

Kooski's heart pounded wildly. He ran
faster than he had ever run in his life.
Another sound rang out. Dirt flew up.
Just inches in front of him.

At last, he stopped behind a rock. He was panting fast. He looked out from behind the rock. He saw something bending over his brother. It held something long in one hand.

It was a sad day in Kooski's life. It was the day he learned about his only enemy. Man.

   45

Chapter 6

The second winter of Kooski's life was very hard. The snow fell deeper than usual. Hunting was difficult.

Sometimes when he woke in the morning, Kooski would be under a foot of snow.

Two of Kooski's siblings had left the pack. They had joined other groups. Or they had mated with lone wolves. Kooski never saw them again.

He had two younger siblings. Both sisters. They were the only ones that had survived out of their litter. A litter of five. Kooski had baby-sat them.

Kooski had caught mice for them. And he had fed the mice to them. Just as the older wolves had done for him. Now his sisters were as big as he was.

In the spring, he would have more brothers and sisters. A new litter would be born. His parents had already dug a new den.

When the new litter was born, Kooski and the older wolves would help take care of them.

The pack was getting large. Some of the older wolves were growing weak.

Food was scarce. Because the winter was so bad. Many deer had died. Even some large elk did not make it.

If any game was caught, it was given to the alpha female first. She needed her strength. For the pups she was carrying.

Many times, Kooski went to sleep hungry. All the wolves did.

Spring came late. The deep snow stayed for a long time.

But finally, it began to melt a little. The wolves were able to catch a few mice.

The new litter was born. But there were only three pups. And one of them lived less than a day. The mother wolf was thin. She was weak from giving birth and going without food.

Very slowly, it got warmer. And the hunting became easier.

One afternoon, the pack killed an elk. It was an elk that had become weak. It would probably have died in a short time.

What a feast the wolves had! They growled and snarled among themselves. As they tore at the meat.

By late spring, the snow was nearly gone. The days grew warmer. The two pups got stronger day by day.

Kooski liked to go off by himself. Sometimes he would go for miles. He would stop often to sniff the air. Kooski had never forgotten the smell of man. The smell of danger.

One morning as he moved along, a new smell came to him. It was a wolf smell. But it was new to Kooski. It was not one of his pack members.

Kooski climbed a little hill. He sat on his haunches and watched.

After a while, a strange wolf came in sight. Kooski could see it sniffing the air. It was a female. A beautiful black female.

Kooski looked in all directions. The female wolf was alone. He went toward her. She backed away.

As Kooski got near, she rolled onto her back. Kooski sniffed her. She tucked her tail between her legs. She licked Kooski's face. Then slowly she got to her

feet. Kooski whined. The black wolf whined.

Kooski came down on his front legs. He wagged his tail. The black wolf wagged her tail.

Then they began to run. Around and around in circles they went. They yipped as they chased each other. For a long time, they played. Then they lay down. Side by side.

At last, the black wolf got to her feet. She bounded off. Kooski raised his nose in the air and howled. Loud and long.

The black wolf stopped. She howled back. Then she disappeared into the woods.

A week later, the two wolves met again. They ran and played together. They hunted together. This continued all summer.

One day in late fall, Kooski left his pack forever. He was going to spend the rest of his life with his mate. The lone black wolf.

They would start a new pack. Kooski would be the alpha male. His mate would be the alpha female.

In the following spring, six pups were born to Kooski and his mate. Two were light buff color. Three were black like their mother. The biggest one was gray like Kooski.

Epilogue

From the 1930s until 1995, there were no wolves in Yellowstone National Park. They were the only animals natural to the area that were missing.

Many times plans were made to put wolves back into the park. Cattle and sheep ranchers fought the plan. They were afraid the wolves would leave the park and kill their livestock.

That would not be a problem, said the conservationists. They said the wolves would eat elk, deer, and other animals found in the park. Their natural food. The wolves would keep the population at a proper balance.

For years, the fight went on. Many surveys were done in the 1980s. Did the public want to see wolves in Yellowstone National Park? The answer was YES! By a margin of 6 to 1.

In January of 1995, 14 gray wolves were released in Yellowstone. The project has been successful so far. It is even operating below the planned budget.

The park now has all the animals and plants that were there when the first white people came to America.

Once more, the call of the wild echoes through Yellowstone National Park.

For more information on gray wolves, contact

North American Wolf Association
23214 Tree Bright
Houston, TX 77373
(281) 821-4884
www.nawa.org